The
Telepathy
Kit

The Telepathy *Kit*

Tara Ward

ARCTURUS

First published in Great Britain by

Arcturus Publishing Limited

First Floor

1-7 Shand Street

London

SE1 2ES

for

Bookmart Limited

Desford Road

Enderby

Leicester

LE9 5AD

This edition published 1999

Printed and bound in the Slovak Republic

60338

Designed by Zeta @ Moo

Illustrations by Neil Puddephatt

© Arcturus Publishing Limited

ISBN 1 900032 44 9

CONTENTS

INTRODUCTION

Telepathy is often linked with the paranormal and given overtones of strange occult happenings. We're going to take a different attitude during this book. We're going to approach telepathy in a much more rational and practical manner.

You're going to be encouraged to relax and to experiment with telepathy, to have some fun with it. In the process, you'll allow your own mind to expand and to embrace a few new concepts which you may not have considered before!

Success with telepathy relies to a large extent on your own ability to relax and to focus your thoughts. Doing both at the same time can take a little practice but the benefits of this spread out into other areas of your life as well. Increasing your capacity to unwind and also to concentrate, can make you much more effective in just about everything you do. This can positively affect your relationships, your demanding job, your exacting role as a parent and running the home, your holiday time and even your search into who you really are. Therefore, practicing telepathy has a number of wonderful side-effects!

Do you know what telepathy is? People often describe it as the ability to read someone else's mind. This is a good starting point from which to work. How on earth is it logical that anyone could read anyone else's mind? After all, we are all individual, we all have our own brain and thought processes. Why should anyone else be able to tap into you?

Have a look at this experiment which was carried out on animals. This is not a theory, incidentally, this actually happened. It has become quite well known as an example of what we might call telepathic abilities and has been given the name *The Hundredth Monkey Principle*.

THE HUNDREDTH MONKEY PRINCIPLE

Behavioural tests on monkeys were carried out by biologist Lyall Watson. He taught a group of monkeys on an island a certain behaviour previously unknown by them. Suddenly another group of monkeys on another island learnt that behaviour, too, *when there was no visible means of normal communication between them.*

On the face of it, an experiment like that seems to be inexplicable. Yet, if you stop to think about it, you have probably had "telepathic" experiences before in your life. Have you ever heard the phone ring and know who was calling you? Have you suddenly felt the urge to contact someone without knowing why and discovered they needed you? Have you ever been in the house wondering where your pet was and had them appear at your side a moment later, as if they knew you wanted them?

These are all examples of you tapping into someone else's wave length and communicating without any obvious, direct vocal, auditory or visual link. So if you didn't see, hear or speak to someone to create this communication, where did you get it from?

The clue lies in relating to people as forms of energy. You are already familiar with physical energy. You know what it is like to feel physically energetic or physically tired. You probably also acknowledge that there is mental and emotional energy, too. There are times when we feel mentally alert and alive and other occasions when our brain feels sluggish and disconnected. Emotionally we can feel uplifted and energetic, too, as well as emotionally exhausted and lacking vitality.

As humans, we tap into each other's energy all the time. We can often tell when someone is energetic or tired. We don't necessarily have to see them for this to take place. We can hear it in their voice or sense it in the energy they give off.

Have you ever walked into a room and immediately sensed an atmosphere? This can work both ways. You can walk into a space and be struck by how lovely it feels. You can also go into an area and feel it is drab or depressing. Again, you don't have to see this to be able to experience it. You could be blind and still be affected by the atmosphere the room has. The same would apply if you were deaf. A prison building has a very different energy from a health centre, which differs again from a school or a factory. Every space reflects what happens within it and who inhabits that area.

Therefore we are coming to the natural observation that people's different energies actually extend beyond their physical body and affect the air around them. Are there people you enjoy seeing because you always feel better for spending some time in their company? Your energies are mingling and creating a healthy environment together. Are there also people you avoid because they leave you feeling tired and irritable? Then your energies are clashing against each other and making you feel uncomfortable.

Have you ever been caught in the crossfire of two people arguing? This can be unnerving as you end up feeling as though you are bombarded energetically from both sides. There is the opposite of that when you find a person or environment in which you feel nurtured and peaceful. This often happens if you treat yourself to a massage or take a moment to commune with nature, whether it be by a walk in the forest or a stroll by the sea or a lake.

So, you can see that we are very much affected by different energies and we do respond differently to what is around us. Now let's go a little deeper and see what might happen with thought processes themselves.

What sort of energy does a thought have? Let's think up an example. Imagine a person sitting alone in a room, thinking murderous thoughts towards someone they believe has harmed them. They are sitting there absolutely furious and full of loathing. What atmosphere have they created? (Remember they are not actually saying or doing anything, merely thinking.) Now imagine that same person sitting there full of love and gratitude for something that has happened in their life. They are feeling wonderful, full of joy and happiness. Would you say there is a tangible difference between the energies that these two thought processes give out? Imagine how you would feel sitting next to the person who is angry, especially if they remained in that state for some time. Now imagine how you would feel being next to the person who is in a joyful state of mind. It would be impossible not to notice the difference.

Below is a pictorial representation of what these two different thoughts might create as far as waves of energy are concerned. Which to you indicates the angry state and which seems to demonstrate contentment?

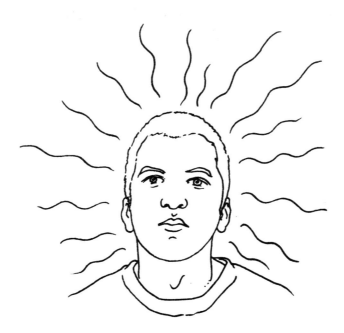

contentment

anger

Therefore, we could follow that concept on to say that every thought carries its own energy and that energy doesn't simply stay within a person's brain but is carried like a wave from the physical body out into the atmosphere. Can you see how we could now reach the stage where we begin to understand how telepathy might work? If every thought has an energy and we respond to different energies, then is it not possible that with training and dedication, we could teach ourselves to acknowledge and to respond to different thoughts from different people?

This isn't as far-fetched as it might first sound. There have been a number of scientific studies carried out on animals to test their behaviour, quite apart from the Hundredth Monkey Principle described earlier. How certain groups of animals seem to know or understand certain behaviours without consciously being taught them has long puzzled scientists and animal behaviourists. This has led many people to the conclusion that animals often possess what we would call telepathic abilities. If animals could speak to us, perhaps they would say that they are merely using their brains in a different way.

You may already know that we as humans only use a tiny portion of our entire brain. Some doctors believe it to be as little as 15%. We know we have the rest of our brain because we need it on some other level, but we have yet to finally determine what that level is. Telepathy may be the opportunity to use that little bit more! Look at the following experiments which have been documented. Again, these are not theories, these are actual results from real tests.

DOG TELEPATHY

A number of different dogs belonging to different owners were left at home alone. Their owners were then asked to vary their returning home time and also to come back via different locations which required a different travelling time. Video cameras were then placed inside the front door of these homes and the dogs were monitored.

A consistently high number of dogs repeatedly go up and went to the door expectantly at the moment when their owners were *thinking* about returning home. Remember, there was no set pattern to the time and location that the owners decided to return home, so the dogs weren't responding to a routine.

BIRD FORMATIONS

It has long puzzled scientists why many species, such as birds, can fly in large numbers, in perfect symmetry, without ever knocking into each other or damaging each other in any way. If you have watched a large display of birds flying closely together, you will understand why some people believe a form of telepathy is taking place. There may be several hundred of them, flying closely together when, as one, they all swoop down and land together. After a number of seconds, they again take off as one and fly in a perfect formation. They can maintain this extraordinary behaviour for long periods of time. (Shoals of fish have also been observed swimming in similar displays of perfect symmetry.) Is there a form of telepathic communication which enables these creatures to perform as though they were but one living force?

Of course, humans also display marked indications of telepathic abilities, as the examples following indicate.

E D G A R   C A Y C E

Edgar Cayce (1877-1945) is probably the world's best known psychic, or telepath. During his lifetime, Dr. Cayce was able to diagnose the illnesses of literally thousands of his patients by going into a deep, trance-like sleep, during which he would telepathically receive information about the nature of a particular patient's ailment. He was not a trained medic himself, he was a professional photographer, so his abilities to diagnose did not stem from any formal training. The preserved records of his work remain and are a solid testament to his extraordinary gifts which have confounded skeptics to this very day. Many books have been published about Edgar Cayce and they make fascinating reading for anyone interested in telepathy.

T E L E P A T H I C   S P Y I N G

Recent years have shown an increasing awareness that various intelligence organisations, such as the CIA, may have been experimenting with telepathy as a means of spying on other countries. A well known example is the book *Psychic Warrior* by David Morehouse which details various allegations of telepathic "spying". Whilst it's difficult to ascertain the accuracy of these accounts, there seems clear evidence that experiments of this nature have been carried out for years behind closed doors in a number of countries.

SHEEP/GOAT EFFECT

Many experiments (quite unrelated to spying) have been carried out with human telepathy over the years, with varying degrees of success. However, parapsychologist Gertrude Schmeidler discovered something particularly helpful during her experiments from 1942 to 1951 which has become commonly known as the sheep/goat effect. Her human subjects were asked, before the experiments with card-guessing began, whether they believed in telepathic abilities or not. Those who believed were called "sheep". Those who disbelieved were called "goats". The results of the experiments which followed over 9 years were logged and analysed. One conclusion was indisputable. *The believers (sheep) consistently scored higher than the non-believers (goats).* Look at the chart on the next page which demonstrates this clearly.

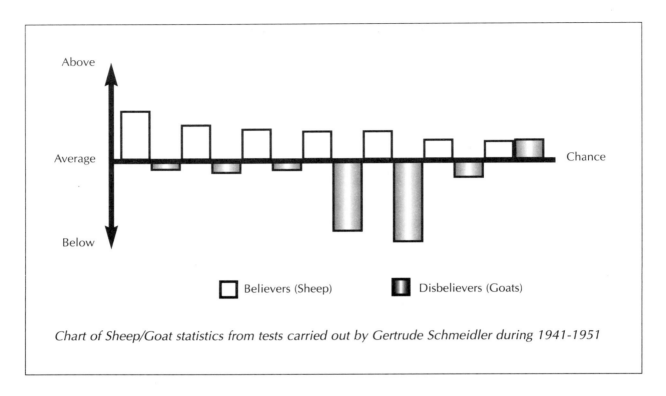

Chart of Sheep/Goat statistics from tests carried out by Gertrude Schmeidler during 1941-1951

You can see by these examples that animals and humans are perhaps capable of more than we realised. What is also very relevant from the last example above, is proof that what we choose to believe very much shapes our abilities to accomplish something. Skepticism often creeps in because, unless something is physically visible, we tend to doubt its existence. The advantage of using telepathy to increase our understanding of greater concepts is that we get instant, visual results with telepathic experiments. We can easily see when we got the desired result and when we imagined something else.

Now let's move on and look at how we need to prepare ourselves so that we can create positive and powerful telepathic experiences!

GETTING READY

WE'VE ALREADY MENTIONED THAT YOU NEED TO BE RELAXED BEFORE YOU START PRACTICING TELEPATHY. Yet many people spend their entire life never stopping to breathe deeply or to focus their thoughts. Especially in our modern western society we are so busy rushing from one over-due task to the other, struggling to fit too much into every day and feeling guilty and stressed when we don't accomplish what we feel we should, that we very rarely take the time just to stop, sit down, breathe deeply and slowly and to really ask ourselves how we're feeling. This process of stopping to assess what is going on in and around you, will enable you to clear the way for successful telepathic experiments. As was mentioned earlier, this relaxation is also going to benefit you in every other aspect of your life as well, so you have nothing to lose and everything to gain from the experience!

True relaxation is only found in deep breathing. How deeply do you breathe when you're unwinding after a long day? Most of us tend to do what is called *shallow-breathe*. This is where we only fill part of our lungs. Our aim is going to be to fill all of our lungs with each breath. Did you know that in our two lungs there are well over a *billion* microscopic sacs called alveoli? These minuscule sacs should inflate and deflate every time we breathe in and out. The majority of us only use a small portion of these sacs because we haven't been taught how to breathe deeply. So let's learn!

To start, place your hands over the front of your ribcage, with your middle fingertips just touching each other. You can sit or stand but make sure your shoulders are back and you are looking straight in front of you. Now take a nice, deep breath in through your nostrils, not your mouth. Are your fingers moving apart? Are your shoulders lifting up? Breathe out again. Are your shoulders dropping? Are your finger tips moving in towards each other again? Look at the diagram on page 18.

You should start in position one. As you breathe in, you should look like position two. As you breathe out, you should revert to position one again. Notice your shoulders should not be lifting at all! Most of us, when we shallow-breathe, try to fill the top half of our body and ignore the rest.

Now try again but this time as you breathe in (through your nose) imagine that you are taking the breath all the way down into your stomach, around your navel area. Imagine that your shoulders have light weights pulling them down towards the ground so that they don't lift up as easily. Slowly let the breath out. Was there a slight difference this time? Keep practicing and every time, think "shoulders heavy, breath to navel". If you feel dizzy at any time, stop! Then resume a little later. You should never strain during deep breathing; it should feel comfortable and relaxing. Once you have spent some time breathing more deeply, you will find it quite easy. Remember to keep practicing!

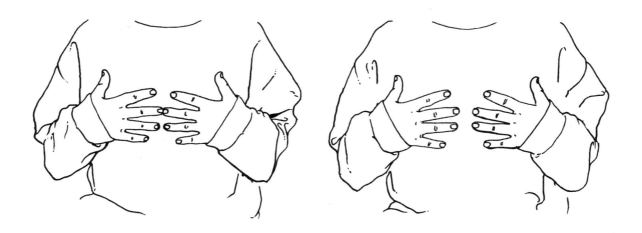

This form of deep, relaxed breathing is wonderful for clearing your mind and refreshing you. Take a minute to breathe deeply at any time during the day when you feel stressed: before an important business meeting, if the children are squabbling, when you're late and stuck in a traffic jam, as you feel an argument brewing with someone, if you're tired, tense, feeling fed-up or depressed. Use your breath as a means to release stress on any level. There is an immediate sense of relief which follows a few minutes of deep breathing and that state can help ease any difficult situation. You may know the expression "count to ten" before doing something. Try taking ten deep breaths instead!

Once you have become accustomed to your deep breathing and enjoyed the benefits of it, then you need to go one step further and learn how to focus your attention. If you can't concentrate and shut out distractions, you will find it hard to work telepathically. There are many methods you can use to help focus your thoughts. Following are a few suggestions.

One very effective method is to concentrate on numbers and use them as a means of focus. You start the exercise by concentrating on your breathing. Close your eyes. When you feel relaxed and comfortable, breathe in and think "10". Breathe out and think "10". Now repeat with the numbers from 9 to 1. The only condition is that while you are on a number, you think of nothing but that number. It's not as easy as it sounds! When you think of 10, for example, you might have your thoughts drift off to a child who is that age or you might think about the number 9 which is coming up. You might also start to think about how long this exercise is taking or what you need to do next or whether you want to rub an itch on your nose. Remember to keep your eyes closed. It is surprisingly difficult to focus all your thoughts on just one thing, whatever it might be. If, during the process, you find yourself thinking about something other than the number itself, then go back to 10 again and start all over again. Don't be surprised if you find yourself returning to 10 a lot in the beginning! Try not to be irritated with yourself if you find it hard initially to concentrate. Just let any unwanted thoughts float away and return to the numbers again. After repeated practice, it does become easier. This is a simple but excellent way to improve concentration.

You might find the symbol of a candle easier to focus upon. It may also appeal to your romantic, softer side which helps you to unwind and to forget every-day stresses. Whatever candle you use, make sure it is in a secure holder and can burn out safely.

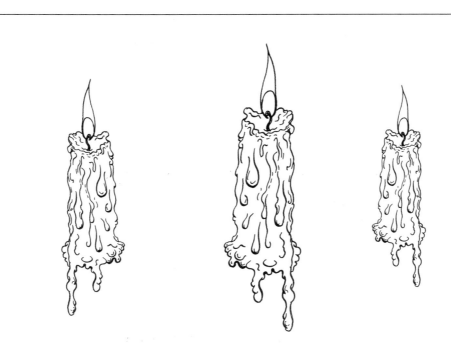

Sit in front of your candle and light it. Breathe slowly and deeply as you gaze at the candle's flame. Focus on relaxing and enjoying the sensation of breathing deeply. Gaze at the candle for a minute or two longer. Try not to blink as you do this. Now close your eyes. You will probably still "see" the candle flame in your mind's eye. That is fine. Now imagine the candle flame coming into the heart area of your physical body. Don't worry if this seems difficult initially. Continue breathing comfortably and relax. Then try again. Let the flame enter into your heart area in your mind's eye. Now be aware of nothing but the candle flame in your heart. This should relax and warm you. It should give you a contented feeling. If you find your thoughts drifting to other matters, let the candle come outside your heart area and then try again. Draw the candle into your heart and let it remain there. See how long it is possible for you to focus on nothing but the candle flame. After practice, it's possible you can remain in that lovely state of relaxation and focus for five or even ten minutes. In the beginning, if you can manage just a minute, you are doing very well! Remember to extinguish the candle when you've finished.

You may find you respond very well to a candle as your means of focus. It is such a nurturing symbol that if often helps the relaxation process. Let's look at one other means of concentration now before we move on to actually working with the cards themselves. This last exercise is really a combination of a relaxation and meditation and is also a confidence-booster! Make sure you have a little time alone when you won't be interrupted for this one. Lock the door if necessary. If you liked working with the candle, have one burning in the room as you work through the exercise.

Work slowly through this exercise and take your time. You need a good ten minutes to enjoy this experience. Sit comfortably and close your eyes. Concentrate on your breathing for several minutes. Breathe deeply in and out, remembering to have your shoulders feeling comfortably heavy and imagining each in-breath being sucked right down into your stomach. Clear any troubled thoughts from your mind. You can have them back again at the end, but during the exercise you might as well relax and let go of them.

Now imagine a point somewhere in the middle of your body. Focus on whatever area you are naturally drawn towards. This may be your heart area, or your solar plexus (between heart and stomach) or even your navel area. Now go deeper into the area you feel drawn to and sink into the "inner you". This is the part of you which knows so much if only you took the time to go into yourself. Whenever you have had your flashes of knowing something without being able to explain why, whenever you have had an indefinable feeling of understanding something on a deeper, more spiritual level, this is where that experience has come from. Keep breathing deeply and let yourself go into that special part of you. On each breath in, feel yourself go deeper into that hidden you.

Remember all the occasions when you have known something without quite working out why. Think of all the times when the phone rang and you knew who it was. Was there a job you knew you were going to get and you did? Did you meet someone and know they were going to be an important love in your life? Think slowly over all the times you have behaved in what might be called a telepathic manner. Think back over what you have learned so far. Remember about how animals respond instinctively to certain scenarios without rational explanation. Think about thoughts being waves of energy into which we can tap. Let yourself be drawn into this new world of discovery and understanding. Keep your breathing deep and regular.

When you feel you have explored as much as you can, slowly bring your awareness back to your physical body. Remember where you are sitting, in which room and what time of the day it is, what day of the week and what you are planning to do next. Open your eyes. Focus on an object and sit still for a few minutes. Make sure you feel relaxed and grounded before you get up.

This exercise can make you feel a little heady. Make sure you give yourself a few minutes to focus again before you get up. If you still feel light-headed when you stand, stamp around the room, feeling how heavy your feet are on the floor. This is a good way to ground yourself. You might be taken aback by the feelings you had during this exercise. Do you now see the possibility of what you are working with? There are energies on a slightly different level from the ones we normally work with, but nevertheless they are present and very real once we learn how to tap into them. Repeat this last exercise several times as you start to work with the cards. Let it give you confidence and a renewed sense of well-being.

Right, now let's get to know the cards!

GETTING TO KNOW THE CARDS

START BY TAKING THE SHEETS FROM THE ENVELOPE AT THE BACK OF THIS BOOK AND PRESS OUT THE CARDS. Once you've done this you will have 16 cards in all which make two identical sets, one blank set and a spare. Place one set on the table in front of you.

At first glance, they appear very simple: a square, a circle, a triangle, a star and two wavy lines. The orthodox method is to shuffle them, choose one and to then "send" that image by thought to someone else. There is nothing wrong with that as an experiment and we'll be doing similar work later with the cards.

However, we're going to take a different approach to begin with and get to know the cards in a more personal way first. The logic behind this is the more you have worked with the cards, the more personal a relationship you have with them, the easier it is for you to tune in to them and to work telepathically. You now know the concept that every thought has a different energy attached to it. Well, we want to create five different energies now, if you like, and allow you to telepathically distinguish between all five.

So let's look at the square first. Take the other four cards away and place the square in front of you. What does a square immediately represent to you? Now take a few comfortable, deep breaths and relax. Look at the square on the card rather as though it were the candle flame; in other words, soften your focus and left yourself melt into the square. If you're relaxed and focused enough, it will probably seem to become something else in front of you. You could say you are letting your imagination take over, or you could say you are actually creating something more from a simple shape. Take your time over this and enjoy the experience. It's meant to be fun, rather than an effort! If you naturally have a good imagination, you'll probably "see" different things in the square. If you're struggling, here are a few suggestions.

Could it become a building, like this?

Here are a few more thoughts to get your creative process working:

  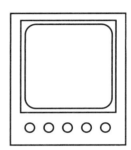

There are so many other items which could immediately spring to mind. Let your imagination run riot and enjoy the process! Make a note or draw any items which you particularly like. You may find the square the easiest because it seems that so many things are that shape.

Now let's move on to the circle. Put the card in front of you and study it. (Do keep the others out of your line of vision or you may become side-tracked.) Again, there are a lot of possibilities. Choose from some of the ideas below, or make up one of your own which feels right for you.

If you enjoy drawing, draw several circles on a piece of paper and then make them into whatever you like. Notice the ones you feel most drawn to. Now you can do the same with the triangle. It may become harder to immediately think of suitable objects but if you stay relaxed and focused, ideas will come to you. How about:

 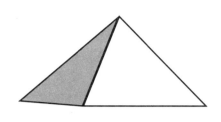 

Are you remembering to keep relaxed and to breathe deeply during this exercise? We often revert back to shallow breathing without realising it. Stop for a moment and take a few comfortable breaths. (You might want to give your shoulders a little shake, especially if you've been hunched over drawing or writing. Blink your eyes a few times to relieve any eye strain.) Now close your eyes for a few seconds. Breathe deeply. When you're ready, open them again and continue.

Now place the star in front of you. So often the only immediate image which comes to mind is a star! However, if you give your imagination free reign, other ideas will come to you. Here are a few thoughts:

(* An interesting extra note here regarding the snowflake and energy flows. Did you know it has been proven that no two snowflakes ever have the identical structure and size? Think of all the snowflakes that have fallen since the beginning of time. Not one of them is the same! It's hard to believe and yet it's true. The more you understand about the extraordinary abilities of nature, the more it makes you realise that humans are likewise extraordinary and wonderful. The only difficulty is that we often forget to take the time to acknowledge that.)

Lastly, we come to the two wavy lines which probably look like - two wavy lines! Place the card in front of you, relax and see what comes to you. The more you get into it, the easier the thoughts flow. Perhaps you got one of the following:

  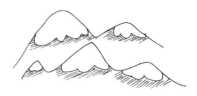

When you have finished playing with the wavy lines, close your eyes for a minute and concentrate on your breathing. Are you sucking the air right down into your stomach area? Are your shoulders nice and heavy? After a minute or two, open your eyes again.

Now you want to go back and look at all five shapes again. Lay them out one after the other, in front of you. Now you want to choose just one image for each symbol. This should be the image or symbol that is the most powerful for you. It should also be the one you like the most! The more you enjoy what you create, the more effective you will be.

So look at the square. What image is most agreeable to you? More importantly, what is the first symbol you see? That now belongs as part of your square. Do the same with the other four cards. It really doesn't matter how silly or frivolous you think the image may be, as long as you're happy. If you love cabbage, make the circle into a cabbage! It doesn't matter. Now you want to keep those images. Make sure they are strong and clear for you. Look at the cards once more. Can you immediately remember what each card symbolises for you? If you're uncertain, you need to go back and repeat the process.

It's a good idea to also have an individual colour to attach to each symbol. Colours are a very powerful way for us to differentiate between energies. If you chose a sun for the circle, for example, choose yellow to go with it. Perhaps your wavy lines are the sea - you might opt for blue as a match. Again, only choose colours you like and enjoy having around you.

When each card clearly means something personal to you and you like the feeling it gives you, then you're ready to move on and do some experiments on your own with telepathy!

SECTION III

WORKING ON YOUR OWN WITH THE CARDS

YOU MIGHT ONLY THINK OF TELEPATHY AS COMMUNICATING WITH OTHER PEOPLE BUT IN FACT YOU CAN PRACTICE ON YOUR OWN FIRST AND GAIN A LITTLE CONFIDENCE!

First and foremost, you want to be relaxed and focused. The more you've been practicing your exercises from Section I, the faster this process will be for you. Take a few moments to clear your mind and relax. Let your worries go. Remember, you can have them back again later! Enjoy the sensation of releasing that stress.

Now pick up your five cards and shuffle them. Don't look down at them as you shuffle. You don't want to be tempted to cheat. Shuffle them for as long as you like and remember to keep your breathing deep and regular and your shoulders comfortably heavy. When you're ready, you want to place the five cards face down in front of you. It doesn't matter how you lie them out as long as they're within easy reach of you. It will probably help you if they aren't in a particular formation. If you like, spread them out in a square shape or circle, for example, it may make you lose concentration and think only of the overall shape of the cards.

Now close your eyes. Focus on the first card you want to find, say the square, and create the image which is associated with it. See the image clearly in your mind's eye. What is the colour that goes with it? See that image and colour vividly in front of you. When you're ready, open your eyes and look down at the five cards in front of you. Which one is your eye drawn to straight away? Try not to strain during this process; the more relaxed you are, the easier it becomes. Enjoy it as a game. If you get it wrong, it doesn't matter. You can try again. Choose one card now.

Were you right? If you were, congratulations! If you weren't, it's not important. Try again! Go through the cards and visualise each one first, then open your eyes and pick the one you feel is right.

How was your success rate first time? Make a note in the chart below:

M Y   F I R S T   A T T E M P T

CARD	SUCCESS RATE
Square	Right / Wrong ✓
Circle	Right / Wrong
Triangle	Right / Wrong
Star	Right / Wrong
Wavy Lines	Right / Wrong

It is interesting to make a note of your first try because it may reveal more than you realise! Which symbols did you get right? Are these the symbols which you like the most and which have the most vivid picture and colour attached to them? Look back at the symbols you got wrong and see whether you have really got to know them as well as the others.

If you got none of them right, it could also be because you aren't as relaxed as you thought. If you got them all right, you're doing wonderfully well!

Irrespective of how well you did, stop and breathe deeply again. Take a moment to find that central core inside of you, which you practiced exploring during the candle exercise. Remember how much there is for you to tap into, energy-wise and how you are now starting to open your mind to other concepts and possibilities. Remember the examples where people and animals apparently knew and understood things without being taught them. Remember you, too, are capable of such things if you relax and focus your thoughts.

Now pick up the cards and shuffle them. As you do so, close your eyes and focus on the card which you believe is your "favourite". This might be because you like the shape or the colour or the image it represents to you. Really focus all your thoughts on this one card. None of the others exist at this time. Remember how you focused on the number exercise such that only one number at a time was in your thoughts? This is the same now. Only one shape, one colour and one image exists in your thoughts. Keep concentrating, but try to relax and to let the thoughts flow. Now stop shuffling.

Keeping your eyes closed, touch the card on the top of the pack with your fingers. Is it the card you are focusing upon? Move it to the bottom and try the next and continue until you have the sensation that you have chosen the right one. Now check the one you feel drawn to. Were you right? Repeat this process using the other four symbols as you continue shuffling the cards. Notice what happened during this second attempt and mark it below:

M Y   S E C O N D   A T T E M P T

CARD	SUCCESS RATE
Square	Right / Wrong
Circle	Right / Wrong
Triangle	Right / Wrong
Star	Right / Wrong
Wavy Lines	Right / Wrong

Can you find a similar pattern to the first attempt? You might find you have improved. Taking the time to slow down further and to relax may have helped you yet again.

Now let's do some further experiments. Take five identical envelopes and place one card in each envelope. Seal them, shuffle them and then number them from 1 to 5. Now either carry the envelopes with you for the day or place them on your desk at work. Think about them from time to time and pick up the envelopes but don't actively try to concentrate too hard on them. (If friends or family around you ask what you are doing, invite them to join in and have a guess, too, but make sure you aren't swayed by their choices.) If at any time, you get a strong feeling that a certain envelope contains a certain symbol, write it down somewhere on the envelope. Change your mind again later, if you like, but you can only change your mind once for each envelope. At the end of the day, you should have at least one symbol for each envelope, or two at the most. Now open the envelopes and see how you "scored". Mark the chart following.

E N V E L O P E   T E L E P A T H Y

CARD	1ST GUESS	2ND GUESS
1	Right / Wrong	Right / Wrong
2	Right / Wrong	Right / Wrong
3	Right / Wrong	Right / Wrong
4	Right / Wrong	Right / Wrong
5	Right / Wrong	Right / Wrong

(If you have a friend who wants to record their results, have them fill in the chart below and then compare your outcomes.)

F R I E N D ' S   E N V E L O P E   T E L E P A T H Y

CARD	1ST GUESS	2ND GUESS
1	Right / Wrong	Right / Wrong
2	Right / Wrong	Right / Wrong
3	Right / Wrong	Right / Wrong
4	Right / Wrong	Right / Wrong
5	Right / Wrong	Right / Wrong

Remember, this is not a competition! It doesn't matter if you got none right while your friend had a high success rate. What it might mean, however, is that your friend might be a good companion when you move on to Section IV and practice with someone else! It's more likely that your friend will have less of a success rate than you, as they haven't had the benefit of your knowledge so far with telepathic work.

How were you drawn to choosing which symbol was in which envelope? Was it through the image which you had devised for the symbol, was it through the original simple shape itself, or was it through the associated colour? Which was the most powerful detective tool for you? Circle what you used for each one in the chart following.

M Y   D E T E C T I V E   T O O L S

CARD	TOOL
Square	Image / Shape / Colour
Circle	Image / Shape / Colour
Triangle	Image / Shape / Colour
Star	Image / Shape / Colour
Wavy Lines	Image / Shape / Colour

Now notice if you had repeated successes with one tool. When you visualised the colour, did you get it right? Perhaps it was your own personal images which came alive for you. You might have found thinking about the symbol itself was more focused and successful for you.

Now compare your successes with your two earlier attempts and notice again if certain symbols were easier for you to choose. Some people find they have more success with the envelope technique. This may be because they are actually straining too much when they sit and concentrate on the cards when they're laid out in front of them. Instead of focusing their thoughts and relaxing, they actually end up feeling quite tense. Did this happen to you? The advantage of having the envelopes and referring to them from time to time during the day is that they can be a momentary diversion from the usual stress of every-day routine. Just taking that short moment to pause and glance at the envelopes, can be the time when you really do relax, both physically and mentally. If you did well with the envelopes, try them again on another day and note your results. Were you quite successful yet again?

This might indicate that you are the type of person who approaches everything in life in a dedicated and focused manner. You are probably already good at concentrating on a given subject and strong on self-discipline. Remember also to give yourself time to unwind. You deserve it!

If you had more success with the first two attempts (and particularly the second) then you are probably already good at relaxing. Your benefit might come from continuing your exercise to focus your thoughts and to improve concentration. If you did well at all three experiments, then you would appear to be well on your way to developing your telepathic abilities!

If you have so far had low positive results in all your tests, it does not mean you are useless and have no telepathic skills! However, it might indicate that you may want to pamper yourself a bit more in the relaxation department. How good are you at finding time for yourself? Are you always giving out to others? Decide that you, too, are worth some time and treat yourself to a massage or have a soak in a long, hot bath. Sit down and read a chapter of that book you've had for ages. Then, gradually, spend a few minutes each day working on your concentration. If you aren't keen on the numbers and candle exercise, then substitute the object for a more pleasing image to you. Spend a few moments listening to your favourite piece of music or close your eyes and focus on your favourite flower or an idyllic holiday spot when you felt wonderful. Use your own thoughts to create a relaxing space in your head. Then you might want to go back over the telepathy exercises in this section and notice your improvement.

Remember, everyone has telepathic abilities. Everyone. It is simply a question of learning how to tap into those other parts of your brain which can access new techniques of awareness - as though your computer has some extra capabilities that you had not yet come across. It can then take you a little while to learn how to use this new part of your computer, but it's wonderful when you master it. Your brain is like that computer and the telepathy is the new skill you tap into. Just allow yourself a little time to adjust to this awareness.

Now let's move on to working on experiments with others. You may find this is where your apparently hidden talents really surface!

WORKING WITH OTHERS WITH THE CARDS

So who would you like to work with on these telepathy experiments? It does matter who you choose. You really want someone who is like-minded to you. They need to have an open, flexible mind and relish new challenges. They should enjoy games and tests. If they also find it easy to relax and possess good concentration skills, you're really on to a winning combination! Both of you will need patience. Working telepathically with others can take some time and you need to be willing not to rush the process.

The best starting point to working together is to share the contents of this book so far with them! (In the early stages, avoid creating images from the symbols with your friend, as you did in Section II. This comes later.) Discuss the necessity of relaxing and focusing. It's a good idea for you to talk each other through the different breathing exercises and concentration exercises. This really benefits you both. Often just talking someone else through an exercise really brings it home to you how beneficial a particular technique can be.

On the next page is a suggested exercise you can speak to each other, just to get you relaxed and focused and ready to experiment. Do make sure you are not going to be interrupted by someone rushing into the room as you go through this. Find time when you can be alone together and then take turns and speak through the following slowly and gently:

SPOKEN EXERCISE

Close your eyes and sit comfortably. Wriggle about if you need to, to make yourself comfortable. Have both feet resting flat on the floor. Take a moment to settle yourself. (Brief Pause)

Now bring your attention to your breathing. On each breath in through your nose, feel the air being sucked right down into your stomach. On each breath out, feel your body becoming more and more relaxed. Your shoulders feel nicely heavy and settled in their sockets. The back of your neck feels loose and comfortable. Whatever problems you have, you are going to let them go during this excercise. Feel them float away into nothingness. Let them go. Just enjoy concentrating on your breathing for a few moments. Continue quietly by yourself. (Pause)

Now every time you breathe in, feel your attention turning inward to the centre of you. To your core. It doesn't matter where this is for you. Your heart, stomach or solar plexus. Focus on the area which feels right for you. Breathe into the stillness which is found in your central core. Enjoy the peace and quiet which exists there. On each breath out, feel the sense of well-being flowing through into all of your body. Let it expand to fill all of you. Enjoy this sensation. Breathe in and focus on your inner self. Breathe out and feel the sensation of peace and calm fill all of you. Continue this way for a few moments. (Pause)

Now, keeping your eyes closed, bring your attention back to your physical body. Notice how heavy your body feels in the chair. Focus on how heavy your feet feel as they rest on the floor. Wriggle your feet and hands a little. Think about which room you're sitting in and what time of day it is. Now open your eyes. Focus on an object. Make sure you feel grounded before you get up.

This exercise is a really enjoyable one to do, even if you're not planning to do any telepathy work! It's so good to feel relaxed and free of stress. Make sure you both read this to each other so both of you get the benefit.

Now give your partner the other set of cards and let them study them. Remember that at this stage, you don't want to go through the process of creating them as images and colours. Let them consider them solely as five symbols. If they want to comment, that's fine, but you don't want to actively associate them as different objects or symbols yet. You're going to work a different way to begin with.

Now you have to decide who is going to be the "Sender" and who is going to be the "Receiver". For the first few attempts, it's suggested that you are the receiver and the other person sends the images to you. This is because you might find initially that you want to send the image of what the symbol has come to mean to you, rather than the simple symbol itself. You want to keep the opening stages of working with someone else as clean-cut and basic as possible.
You can go into separate rooms if you want to avoid the possibility of cheating and seeing the other person's cards. However, a very effective way is simply to sit back-to-back, making sure no mirrors face either one of you. Make yourselves comfortable in the chair. Have both feet resting firmly on the ground and breathe deeply.

Now the Sender is going to pick up their five cards and shuffle them for a while. Ensure that they use the second set of cards which you have kept in the back of this kit. The Receiver just sits, closes their eyes and relaxes, while the Sender shuffles their cards and relaxes and focuses their own thoughts. When the Sender is ready, they tell the Receiver they are going to start.

The Sender then stops shuffling and turns over the top card. They then say something like "I am now sending you the first card". They do this by focusing only on that one image. Nothing else should come into their thoughts. They may want to imagine sending that image out on a wave of thought to the Receiver. They may imagine a beam of light connecting them to the other person and beam the image down the line. They may have their own personal thought process which works for them. How they choose to do this isn't important at all. What does matter is being relaxed and focused. Those are the two keys to success. If either one of you is straining or struggling, it will create a block in the energy between you.

The Receiver need do nothing but clear their mind of any thoughts and have a large blank canvas in front of their mind's eye. Then they wait for the image to manifest itself in front of them. The more "empty" and relaxed they are, the more they will be in a state to receive the information. The important aspect for the Receiver is not to pre-empt any information by imagining a symbol for themselves. The image is not to come from them, but be received by them as an energetic thought form.

Initially, the Sender will probably feel as though they aren't working hard enough and the Receiver will keep wondering if they are imagining the symbol for themselves! Don't spend a long time on any card. Just focus your thoughts for a minute or so and then move on. Make sure the Sender says "I am now concentrating on the second card". The Receiver might want pen and paper to make a note of the symbols in case they forget the order. Work through all five, without telling each other which symbol is which and then compare the results at the end, filling in the chart below.

W O R K I N G   T O G E T H E R - 1st Time

SENDER'S NAME	RECEIVER'S NAME
SENDER'S CARD	RECEIVER'S IMAGE
1	1
2	2
3	3
4	4
5	5

Whatever results you got, discuss how both of you felt. When you got one right, did it feel stronger as an image than the others? Did the Sender or Receiver change their tactics in any way through the experiment? In other words, did the Sender change the way they were sending the image or did the Receiver relax and focus more half-way through the proceedings? Is either one of you particularly fond of one shape or do you particularly dislike a certain symbol? Were you both somewhat nervous? Did you allow enough time for each symbol? Don't worry if your results are disappointing to you. Congratulations if you're pleased!

Now repeat the whole experiment but change positions. The Receiver becomes the Sender and vice versa. Use your own cards for this. Don't change cards over as they become personal for you. Remember, if the Sender is the person who has been working for a while with telepathy, they must only send the shape for the purposes of this experiment. Do not send a symbolic representation or any colour. This will only confuse the Receiver.

After you have tried this experiment once, you might want to be a little more specific in this second attempt. You might decide you will use just one method of sending the image, for example. You might like to create a pipe of energy between you which the image can flow down. Or you might choose a laser of light.

The Receiver might decide they will imagine themselves to be more open and receptive. They might want to create their own form of energy connection such as imagining a hole in the back of their head connecting to the back of the other person's head.

Each of you use your own imagination and create what feels right for you. You don't have to share the image at this stage. Wait until the second experiment is complete before you discuss it. When you've finished, note your results below.

WORKING TOGETHER - 2nd Time

SENDER'S NAME	RECEIVER'S NAME
SENDER'S CARD	RECEIVER'S IMAGE
1	1
2	2
3	3
4	4
5	5

Were the results better this time? Or were they worse? How different did the two of you feel during this second attempt? Now really discuss how it felt for each of you and what method of communication you were trying to create. Is there common ground for creating a similar tool of energy between you? Discuss what feels right for both of you and find a way that is similar which suits both of you. Don't be afraid to discuss any idea, no matter how silly it might sound. Are you both fascinated by UFOs and aliens? Create a "messenger" which beams their way from one to the other! Do you both like being by or on the water? Create a fast flowing stream which carries the energy from one person to another. Perhaps you love astrology and want a special star to carry the information between you. Anything goes, anything is fine, so long as you both agree on the method. Also, make sure whatever you choose acts as a compliment to and not a distraction from the telepathy. You don't want to get so caught up creating a complex web of energetic communication, such that you forget to focus on the shape itself!

When you are clear about how you want to communicate and both of you feel happy about this, then try the experiment again and concentrate solely on the agreed means of connection between you. Then notice the results again.

W O R K I N G   V I A   C O M M O N   G R O U N D

SENDER'S NAME	RECEIVER'S NAME
SENDER'S CARD	RECEIVER'S IMAGE
1	1
2	2
3	3
4	4
5	5

If you want to repeat it yet again and swap over the Receiver and Sender then do so and notice the difference. It will also start to become clear to you, that one person is better at being a Sender than another. This is natural. Most people are better at one than the other. Once you discover which works best for you, stay with that combination for a while and notice your progress.

When you feel ready, you might want to try varying your approach. Now we're going to have you both using a set of five cards each and experiment with how you might tune in to each other's wave length via the cards. For this you will need a small table each. Again, you should have your backs to each other and avoid any temptation to cheat! (You can also do this via the telephone, or, if you prefer, write down your separate results and then post, fax or email them to each other. However, most people feel more secure if they're in the same room. The close proximity makes them feel it's easier to tap into each other's thoughts and psychologically makes them feel more confident.)

So now you want to take your five cards each and sit back to back again, this time with a small table in front of each of you. Remember to relax, sit quietly, concentrate on your breathing and focus your thoughts. You want your telepathic energies to flow easily and smoothly. When you're both ready, each take your five cards and lay them face up in front of you. Lie them out in a straight line. Next, you both want to choose just one card, without telling the other person what it is. Say to each other "now" as you do this. Put it to one side. Then go back to your other four cards. Which one do you want to pick up next? When you're both ready, say "now" and each pick up the second card. Repeat this process until all five cards have been chosen. Make sure you are clear about the order in which you chose them, from one to five. Now record your results.

WORKING WITH BOTH SETS OF CARDS

MY RESULTS	FRIEND'S RESULTS
1	1
2	2
3	3
4	4
5	5

Was this more successful for you? Sometimes, when both of you are more "active" it makes you more confident. Did you both choose quite quickly and did it seem easy to pick each card? Try this experiment several times and notice how efficient you are. Always remember to keep creating whatever line of communication you have agreed upon.

You can also try both of you laying out the five cards and the Sender just sending the image of one of the cards to the Receiver. The Receiver simply relaxes and gazes at the five cards in front of them. They may find that one of the cards seems to sort of "jump" out at them and they feel the urge to choose it. It sometimes feels as though one card is particularly bright or that it is pulsing with energy or that it has a light over it. Both of you could try receiving this way and see whether it works for you.

Once you have worked through all these experiments, then you might consider going slightly deeper and working via the images, like the ones you first created yourself in Section II. This can get more complex and confusing, of course, for both of you, requiring heightened attention and focus. It's not suggested that you try this until you have worked a number of times with the other experiments detailed in this section. However, when you're ready, it can be an enjoyable change to try what follows.

You now want to introduce your friend to the work you did during Section II. Explain how each shape can be likened to some image which feels relevant for them. Explore the shapes again, together this time, and notice what new contributions your friend has to make. There are always new possibilities through someone else's imagination being added to your own! Take each card separately and enjoy letting your imaginations run riot. Discuss whatever silly or wild idea you have for each, but remember the shape must always be relevant to the symbol you create. When you have fully expanded your thoughts for each of the five symbols, then you can try the test below.

Again sit back to back with a table in front of you and agree upon the one symbol which you will work upon. Whatever you choose, place that card face up somewhere on your table. Now take a sheet of A4 paper each and a pen or pencil. Each draw the shape on the paper. Now, when you're both relaxed and ready, agree that you will draw whatever image comes onto that shape and try to work in tune with each other. Don't rush this process and don't confer over what you are actually drawing. Just take your time and remember to keep the lines of communication flowing between you. Don't make it a great effort, either. It doesn't matter if what you draw bears no relation to your friend as it's only an experiment. Make sure as you work that you are continually keeping in touch with your friend's energy. You don't want to get wrapped up in your own world and forget the other person. The idea is to synchronise your thoughts so that a pleasant harmony ensues. Keep drawing until you feel the urge to stop, irrespective of what the other person is doing. Then compare your works of art.

Are they completely different?! Have a laugh and try again on another day. Are they similar images but drawn very differently? For instance, you both might have drawn a sun for the circle shape but they could have turned out like this:

The fact that you chose to draw the same object, albeit in two very different ways demonstrates that you were both thinking in the same way during the exercise. Repeat this with all the other symbols and see what similarities you can find. Often you may find you have the same idea in mind but your own personalities allow you to draw this very differently.

If you both find this drawing process is a powerful medium for you to work in then why not increase the tools you use to work with? You can try adding coloured pencils into the equation (as long as you both have identical sets of crayons) and see if you choose similar colours when drawing. Decide you will choose whatever size you want to draw, so you can fill the whole page or just use a tiny corner with your chosen shape. How often do you both draw in the same size?

Is there an emotion affiliated to each drawing? After you finish your artwork, agree you will each write an emotion or feeling connected to the drawing. Are your emotions often connected, even if the drawing is very different?

Always remember to have the basic card itself on the table in front of you as you work. It is always your initial inspiration and represents your starting point. After you have worked with the drawing for a while, then return back to the original telepathic exercises and Send and Receive the original symbols again to and from each other. You might find images creeping in as well from all your other exercises. Always discuss how you felt afterwards and observe how your methods have changed. Make a note of your results this time around and see if your success rate has become higher now.

Whether your results have improved or not is really unimportant. What matters are the benefits you feel you have enjoyed as a result of the experiments. Have you embraced this opportunity to relax and focus your thoughts on something other than your normal, day-to-day pressures and worries? Have you and your friend had a good laugh together? Have you discovered more about each other in the process? Do you feel you are more open and receptive to what is around you, as a result of experimenting with these five simple cards? In our last section, we are going to look at how we could work even deeper with telepathic abilities and how we can use them constructively and enjoyably to help enrich many areas of our life.

SECTION V

GOING FURTHER

THIS LAST SECTION IS ABOUT DELVING INTO TELEPATHY ON A DEEPER LEVEL. You might look at this and decide it's not for you and you would rather continue your experiments on the level you have already been working. That is fine. Why not try all the experiments over again in Section IV but choose another friend this time? Chances are the results will be very different as each individual is so different. Some people are naturally more in tune with each other and it takes less focus and less effort to create positive results. Only by experimenting will you discover what and who works best with you.

So how can we work deeper with these five cards and their symbols? What else is there to discover? We're going to go back to the basic five symbols and see what else there is to learn about the significance of these shapes, in other words, what they might mean to us individually and what we could glean from them that might positively impact on other areas of our life. We're going to use these symbols to access higher thoughts and concepts and to make us question certain aspects of life. Does it sound impossible that five symbols could possibly teach us anything about life? Read on!

To start this process, you need a little quiet time to yourself. Just before you drift off to sleep is ideal, as our brain patterns often shift as they prepare for sleep. That shift can often open other areas of awareness within ourselves, if it is channelled properly. We'll work through the symbols one at a time, to help you look at what you might learn from each.

Before you go to sleep one night, choose one of the cards and place it on your pillow or bedside table. When you get into bed, look at the card for a moment or two. Relax, breathe deeply and focus on what the symbol means to you if you consider it in a larger context. Below are some ideas to inspire you and to help you move along this new path.

T H E   C I R C L E

What in life is represented by a circle? You may have already created thought-provoking objects such as the world and the sun through earlier work. These planets and others are endlessly circling and orbiting in space. A circle has no beginning and no end. It is constant.

What in your life represents constancy and cycles of repetition? Do you find these areas nurturing or stifling? Keep thinking about circles of events and situations. Have you created certain scenarios in your life which you constantly repeat over and over? Do these cycles leave you feeling complete or do they leave you frustrated and confused? What can you find in your life which is comforting which you know belongs to a regular cycle of events or conditions? Who do you see as controlling the circles you don't like? Are there areas in your life where you have the ability to change these circles but you have yet to take the responsibility for this happening?

Finish the thought process by acknowledging the areas in your life which do provide great comfort and security and be appreciative of these. As you drift off to sleep, keep the image of the circle in your thoughts. Have a pen and pad by your pillow so that as soon as you wake up in the morning, you write down the thoughts which came to you in the night that relate to the circle.

T H E   S Q U A R E

Prop the square up next to you one evening. The square often represents solidity, a secure box-like shape which is very familiar. What areas in your life feel secure and solid? Do you like putting sections of your life into different boxes which keeps them separate? For instance, is your relationship with your family different from that with your friends? Is work very separate from your home life? Do you prefer areas of your life to be self-contained or would you like some of the contents of those boxes to be merged together? How many different boxes are there in your life?

What about other boxes that might be there for you, but remain unopened? Imagine some other boxes in your mind's eye now. What might they contain which could enrich your life? Do you want to open them or do you feel nervous about how they might alter your present life?

Finish your meditation by appreciating the positive boxes in your life which afford you stability and support your own personal needs. Drift off to sleep with the image of the square firmly in your head and make a note in the morning of any dreams which seem relevant.

THE STAR

Put the star on your pillow. Have you spent time just looking up at a starry sky and wondering about how far away those twinkling lights really are? What do you feel when you think about time and space and where our planet Earth is in relation to all those bright stars?

Do certain aspects of life seem far removed from your own reality? Are there people or situations that you keep at arm's length because you are frightened to get too near, in case you are burned by them? What in your life seems so far away from you that you are sure it would never approach and influence your own life? What would you like to have closer to you, to offer you a richer enjoyment of life?

Put those wishes on a star and then watch that star coming closer to you. Realise that there are many stars of opportunity around you in the world and that you can call upon them when you want to. What stars are already shining brightly around you and which nurture you now? Drift off to sleep with these in your thoughts and visualise many bright, twinkling stars all around you. When you wake, jot down whatever happened in the night that feels important.

T H E   W A V Y   L I N E S

Look at the wavy lines as you get into bed one night. They express a certain fluidity and synchronicity just by their shape and symmetry. Are there two areas of your life which flow along harmoniously together? Add more wavy lines in your mind, if there are more than two areas which you feel work well together.

What would you say naturally flows along in your life which you can observe and enjoy, as opposed to fret over? What areas of your life have become too wavy and flow too quickly? How does that make you feel? What areas in your life seem to refuse to flow smoothly? What are the blocks which stop them from flowing? Have you created these "dams" yourself or are they from other people? What can you do to free the blocks and allow your life to flow harmoniously? How does your body and mind feel when your life flows freely and easily?

Finish off by appreciating all the areas in your life which flow freely. Then let yourself fall into sleep with the sensation of soft, undulating waves. When you wake, make a note of what you experienced during the night.

T H E   T R I A N G L E

The triangle represents three sides to existence. We often say certain things are three-fold, meaning 3-dimensional, as opposed to flat. Do you feel your life reflects a full 3-dimensional picture? Do you feel you embrace all experiences and possibilities with enthusiasm and open-mindedness? What areas in your life seem to be three dimensional and fully enjoyable from all sides? Are there pockets of your life which seem to be flat and one-dimensional? What would it take to reshape them into 3-dimensional experiences?

You've probably been told that "good things come in threes". Where is there a trio of happiness in your life? We often group things together into three such as "the sun, the moon and the stars", the "3R's" or "3's a crowd". Where is 3 significant in your life? Where is it missing?

Finish by picturing your life as a complete 3-dimensional image, which contains all that is necessary for a fulfilled existence. Drift off to sleep with that image. Let the triangle drift off with your thoughts. When you awake, scribble down any relevant issues which came up in your dreams.

Are you beginning to see how these symbols can have some meaning in other areas of your life? Let yourself work at this level with these symbols for a few weeks. Enjoy what you discover. Always remember to let any final thoughts which you have be nurturing, positive images.

You might want to share this experiment with your friend and see what they discover, or you may feel it is too personal and that you would rather keep the experience to yourself.

If you do want to work with someone else via dreams, you can try sending each other a positive image or thought at a certain time of the evening or night. Make sure whatever you send is nurturing in content. Many people find working via dreams are powerful because the body and mind are often so relaxed that they let certain energies flow freely.

You might feel that working on your own with the symbols at night is not really telepathy and has nothing to do with telepathic abilities. However, working telepathically basically means opening your thoughts and mind to other, higher processes. You're just using what you were born with (your brain) in a slightly different way to access information.

Once you start to work telepathically, all sorts of other openings are suddenly created for you. You begin to understand yourself and others in a deeper, more appreciative way. Empathy and sympathy suddenly seem natural states of being. You will probably notice from your experiments with your friend, that you seem to be closer in other ways through this. You might be more in tune with their emotions or daily events in their lives, without quite understanding why. It's perfectly natural. You are developing communication between you and it will impact your relationship in a wonderfully helpful way. You will start to notice how everyone basically has their own energy and feel to them. This includes animals and plant-life and all forms of nature. Even inanimate objects have a distinct energy with which you can link telepathically.

Have you lost your favourite watch or pen? Just spend a moment relaxing and focusing your thoughts. Concentrate on the object you have lost. Where is it now? Trust that the energy is there somewhere for you to tap into if you simply take a little time and practice to make it work.

Telepathy is a starting point from which you can expand your thoughts. Enjoy using the cards in this kit. Go through various exercises again and share them with as many people as possible. Have a laugh as you experiment and don't worry if you can't match your results all the time. Use your imagination and make up your own, personal telepathic experiments. You might find they work very well for you.

Lastly, you will notice there are also some blank cards in this kit. These are for you to use in whatever way is right for you. You aren't going to be guided and instructed on what to do with them because they're meant as individual tools for you. Use them to draw your own images and then work with them on your own, or with others. What different aspects of your life can you delve into and gain a deeper understanding of, through the new images you draw for yourself? Remember, they can be private thoughts, if you like, and you don't have to share them with others. It's fine for telepathy to be an individual experience. Just make sure, whatever your experiment, that you always finish on a good note, acknowledging yourself for all the positive aspects of your life.

As you enjoy your telepathy cards, both the printed ones and the ones you draw on yourself, remember to let that sense of pleasure and fun spread out into other areas of your life. Everything in life can be explored with an open and inquisitive mind. Nothing should be a struggle and effort forever. Enjoy the process of sharing what you have learnt with others. As you relax and play with telepathy, also take a moment to remember that you can have freedom and fun touch all areas of your life!